Spot the Shape

Shapes in Art

Rebecca Rissman

Heinemann Library
Chicago, Illinois

Designed by Joanna Hinton-Malivoire
Photo research by Tracy Cummins and Heather Mauldin
Colour Reproduction by Dot Gradtions Ltd, UK
Printed and bound by South China Printing Company Ltd

13 12 11 10 09
10 9 8 7 6 5 4 3 2 1

Library of Congress Cataloging-in-Publication Data
Rissman, Rebecca.
Shapes in art / Rebecca Rissman.
p. cm. -- (Spot the shape!)
Includes bibliographical references and index.
ISBN 978-1-4329-2169-9 (hc) -- ISBN 978-1-4329-2175-0 (pb) 1. Shapes--Juvenile literature. I. Title.
QA445.5.R57 2008
516'.15--dc22
                          2008043206

Acknowledgments
The author and publishers are grateful to the following for permission to reproduce copyright material: ©Alamy pp. **4** (Freefall Images), **15** (1), **16** (1), **23b** (1); ©Bettina Strenske pp. **17**, **18**; ©Heinemann Raintree p. **21** (David Rigg); ©Jupiter p. **6** (Robert Harding Images/Jane Sweeney); ©Jupiter Images pp. **11** (Corbis), **12** (Corbis); ©Shutterstock pp. **9** (Michael Rubin), **10** (Michael Rubin), **13** (Zeber), **14** (Zeber), **19** (Franck Boston), **20** (Franck Boston); ©The Bridgeman Art Library International pp. **7** (The Trustees of the Goodwood Collection), **8** (The Trustees of the Goodwood Collection), **23a** (The Trustees of the Goodwood Collection).

Cover photograph of Factories, 1926 (oil on card) reproduced with permission of ©The Bridgeman Art Library International/Seiwert, Franz W. (1894-1933)/ Hamburger Kunsthalle, Hamburg, Germany. Back cover photograph of diamond pattern cloth reproduced with permission of ©Jupiter Images/Corbis.

Every effort has been made to contact copyright holders of any material reproduced in this book. Any omissions will be rectified in subsequent printings if notice is given to the publisher.

Contents

Shapes

Shapes are all around us.

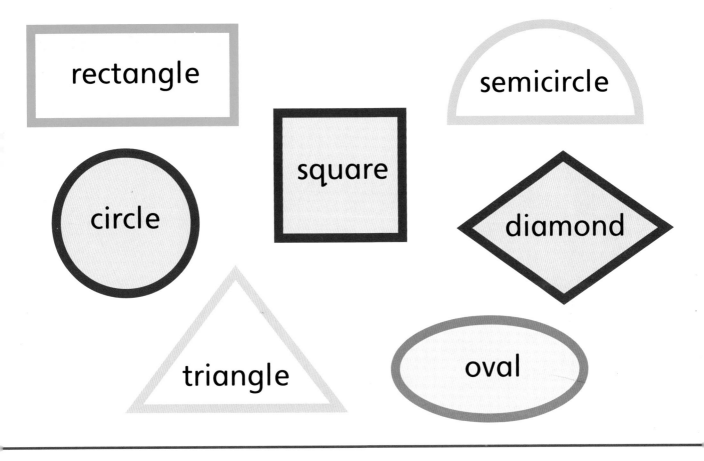

rectangle

semicircle

circle

square

diamond

triangle

oval

Each shape has a name.

Shapes in Art

There are many shapes in art.

What shape is this picture frame?

This picture frame is an oval.

What shape is the cherry on this sculpture?

The cherry on this sculpture is
a circle.

What shapes are in this cloth?

Diamonds are in this cloth.

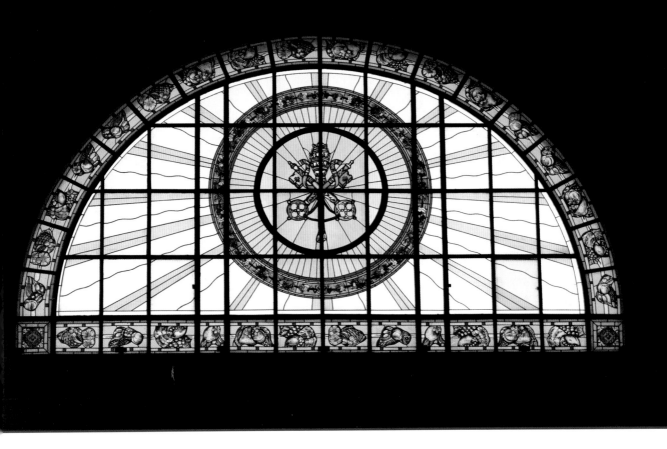

What shape is this window?

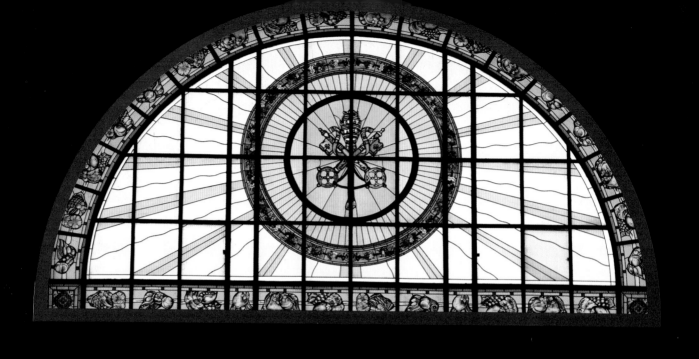

This window is a semicircle.

What shape is in this sculpture?

A rectangle is in this sculpture.

What shape is this man painting?

This man is painting triangles.

What shapes are in this sculpture?

There are squares in this sculpture.

There are many shapes in art.
What shapes can you see?

Naming Shapes

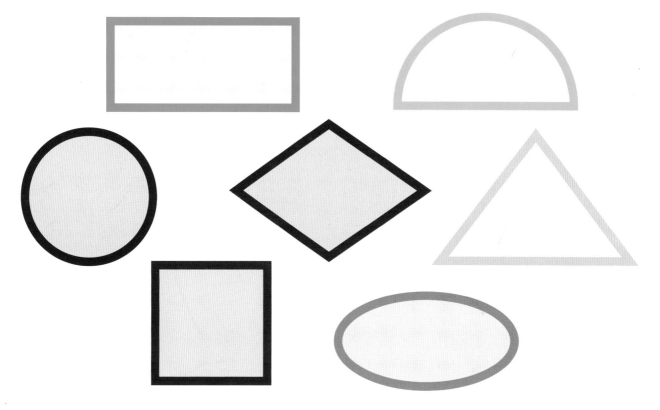

Can you remember the names
of these shapes?

Picture Glossary

frame piece of wood or metal around the edge of a picture

sculpture model that an artist carves or makes out of material like stone, wood, or clay

Index

Note to Parents and Teachers

Before reading

Write a list of geometric descriptions on the board (for example, straight lines, three corners, curved, four sides). Give each child one large shape cut from cardstock. Ask each child to write descriptions of their shape on the cardstock.

After reading

- Make a shape person: cut different shapes from colored cardstock. Then show children how to make a person out of shapes. Show them how to use a circle for the head, a square for the body, two larger rectangles for the trousers, smaller rectangles for the arms and legs, and small squares for the feet. Invite children to get creative and use as many shapes as they can think of.
- Shape search: take children on a shape search around the school grounds or around the classroom. Give each child a cut-out shape and ask him or her to find a matching shape. Make a class list of all the shapes they find.